T0106552

AuthorHouse™
1663 Liberty Drive
Bloomington, IN 47403
www.authorhouse.com
Phone: 1-800-839-8640

First published by AuthorHouse 8/25/2009

ISBN: 978-1-4490-1419-3 (sc)

Printed in the United States of America
Bloomington, Indiana

This book is printed on acid-free paper.

authorHOUSE®

GHET-TO

LOVE

YOURSELF

WRITTEN
BY
PHYLLIS WASHINGTON

Dedication

I would like to dedicate this book to
all of the pain.

Because without it I would not of been able to
Ghet-to love myself

This book also is dedicated to
my

Parents
Sister
Sons
Daughters

Who have experienced Ghetto Love

Hindsight

Twenty Twenty
Vision
(George Benson)

If I knew then what I know now, perhaps their would have been less pain and agony in my youth. I hope this book will help the thousands of couples, and singles to miss out on all of the unnecessary burdens of having to jump over the hurdles that life had brought my way.

One way to receive hindsight is to go to the mature, experienced ones around you who have already gone through what you have yet to experience.

Where are these experienced ones?, Like most blessings they are right in front of you. A dad, mom, grandparents, aunt, uncle, and sometimes it could be a brother or a sister.

We need to tap into these sources for hindsight. Does it matter whether they have lived during your lifetime or somewhere in the past, no just take time our ask questions, be observing, and listen with your heart and with your mind.

And you'll receive
Hindsight

Table of Contents

Chapter One

Let's get Physical
(Olivia Newton John)

Do we ever really get to know the person we so freely fall in love with or do we, fall head over heels in love with the first glance, at their eyes, the way they twinkle, or the way their lips curl a certain way when they smile?

Could it be the way a person is shaped physically, for me it was the eyes, why? Well I just couldn't see what other men saw in me, maybe if I saw it first it wouldn't have been such a lure of attraction. Somehow a man could make me feel good or bad by the way he looked at me, I know it may sound silly, or, maybe that is the way God meant us to be in order to be drawn to one another

but...

do we take it to a much higher level than was originally intended? Well I know it was that way for me. It's not that I didn't have some of the same vanities that the next person had, what I mean is, I could go to the closet pick out an attractive outfit, groom my hair, put on my make up and shoes. Like my daughter Eisha expressed to me a couple of summers ago when I expressed how well she dressed, she commented that she never would go out in just anything, but I still didn't feel the appropriate amount of self esteem.

The reason I want you to feel me is because this was a very dangerous pattern I developed. As you continue to read you'll come to see where I developed these low self esteem issues. You see once I so called gave over my power to these men, they controlled my every breathe, my very existence.

You see if they didn't show their approval for the day, my day was shot. In a moment or a twinkling of an eye I could go from feeling truly happy, faithful, domestic, business oriented, able to handle the world, to a helpless, and afraid, numb little girl.

This would go on for years I'd be in the grip of Getting Physical.

Never realizing this was happening to me you may ask how did this affect my faith? This was suppose to be the strongest part of us and yet, I may have blamed God for all of the disappointing things in my life. Especially my relationships. When we expect another human being to give us what we should seek from God, that's only asking for a let down.

We are exactly that, human beings with imperfections and dysfunctional patterns. Yes, bring two people together who have been beaten, frightened, molested, abandoned by parents in a drunken rage. This type of relationship is doomed right from the start. These couples fall into each others arms exhausted from life, having literally been persecuted, sometimes from birth.

We had deep emotional scars that we either buried or express violently, tearfully and depressed. This is so hard for me to write about myself, because the scars are and forever will be their, but... I choose today how much of my past I will allow myself to dwell on and even then only if I feel their is something I can better understand about myself.

How did my ghetto lover affect my domestic duties, well have you ever done something for someone and not felt appreciated?, Well that's what I have experienced. I think back and understand that, you can't be validated b someone who has never been validated themselves.

In the ghetto for whatever reasons our parents hadn't been given the tools needed to rear and properly train children emotionally, I mean my mother made sure of the basics, food, clothing, ect..., but I can't remember her ever sitting with me reading a book or all of those other things such as, baking cookies, now that I recollect I didn't have a baked chocolate chip cookie till I was at least eight or nine years of age when I went to camp. Whoa!!! this just blew me away, see my grandmothers were dead by the time I was born so basically their was no mothering or grand mothering, so quite naturally all of this affected my domestic side.

My relationships also affected my sense of business. Many of the boyz in the hood didn't have father figures or shall I say male role models in the home. Yeah some did, ok but, many didn't. I have to admit many of parents weren't focusing on bills there just wasn't enough in the bi-weekly financial assistance, most people work and earn enough to pay bill, buy a house, a car and save for their children's education.

but... the economic status of that time was very poor for the people of the ghetto.

I don't ever want to be caught making excuses for us but, I found it very hard to obtain a job where I felt mentally able to hold and keep a job. I've had many jobs, but found that I lacked the self confidence to hold my jobs as did many. The majority of us were products of a system that had kept us oppressed mentally, emotionally, and this didn't allow us the stamina needed to go from the projects to the outside world, where we were discriminated against for the color of our skin our flesh.

Just looking others of the white race in the eyes was met with an air or superiority. This gets weary on the body, and is very draining to us especially our young men who were treated less than.

In other words the domino affect of society trickled down form one generation to the next, from generation to the next, from one status in life to the lowest poverty level. All of these composites during ones ignorance can allure you in so many directions and mistakes in life, work, and in choosing a mate. Just by seeing the physical, yeah, just getting physical.

Chapter
Two
Papa was a Rolling Stone
(The Temptations)

My dad's passed on now, but he still lives in my daily thoughts I guess it would only be fair to look at his - story to really be able to understand what has happened to him and also what made him who he was.

I sure can't take away from him, his style I mean his hair, dress, the way he held his cigarette, or the cars he drove, whenever he came to see us. Even though we didn't have much, I never wondered why he seemed to look so well taken care of, while we seem to move so often after THE-MAN sat at the table with my mom and left her in tears.

Now, looking back I realize she was being put out again, but she never mentioned what she was going through to us. She was very courageous, trying to raise us two girls alone.

Sometimes we as young adults or children don't realize how much our parents sacrifice for us. Now that I recollect about those times, it was so much easier for the parent that departed, he'd come and go when he pleased. Went to work without having to worry about who'd care for the children.

Dad never stayed nowhere or with no one to long. I mean he had many women that would fight to take him in and he knew it. He was charming, cool, and always had a pocket full of money, but why shouldn't he, their were no bills to pay, rent, light, oil, phone, school clothes, college tuition no, just himself to take care of.

A rolling stone, if a stone breaks off from a mountain and rolls down, it will crush and destroy anything in its path, without any remorse or regrets, I mean a stone has no feelings.

That's what happened to my family we were crushed and almost destroyed

by

PAPA

CAUSE

"Papa was a rolling stone"

My childhood was spent mostly with my mother, it

seemed as though I seen my father maybe two weekends a month, sometimes one. It was as though chasing women was his major concern, this made me feel awkward, not jus him but, many brothas then and even today make chasing women their number one goal in life. As a child of a player this meant he couldn't behave around the opposite sex, even just a hello from the opposite gender would send the wheels rolling. Whether we were at a family gathering, picnics, cookout, schools, neighbor, and especially on the job. I can't tell you the embarrassing predicaments dad put me in. Well I knew he was married, Hell she was my mother!

Still he had no regard for her or my feelings, sometimes he'd swear me to secrecy in one of his little escapades at one of his girlfriends house. I thank God that my mother didn't question me, because I didn't like lying one bit.

I mean the audacity to disrespect our entire family, then came the half brothas, and more secrecy. I'm grateful to have met my brothers, but unknowing to them my mother went through a hell of a nightmare. Always wondering where her husband was, where was he wearing his satin two piece suit to every weekend. I remember praying for nearly one to two years, I had faith that one day God would reunite our family, but God was trying to protect me from my fathers ghetto ways, and when the weekend came he was gone, but not until they had a good battle of words, yelling, and hitting. God knew, that my dad wasn't the settling down type, but I didn't, and I was praying and begging for their reuniting but, I had a rude awakening.

Those were peculiar times in the ghetto, relationships hardly had a prayer. You had your daddy running after anything in a skirt, mommy drinking and crying because he was, so that left us kids running wild in the projects just, playing basketball, playing in the sprinklers when it got hot, waiting on the ice cream truck and daddy to come back. They both were a well needed treat. Which is easier taking care of and loving one set of children and a wife?, or taking care of two or three families. I mean we all wanted some ice cream, where the hell was dad. I couldn't even get money for the penny store from moms, shoot she had enough to feed us, clothe us every three to six months and the rest was for her medication, if you know what I mean. I mean after you have one drink your smooth, mellow even, but if you feel that you need two to three bottles of Wild Irish Rose, or straight up Vodka, what the hell are you trying to forget?

Well if you were my mother maybe it was her dream of one day owning a home with my dad, taking rides with him in his new cars while in his satin suits, or maybe going to the salon for a new due, or traveling some where exotic, or just us being together as a loving family, but daddy had other dreams and they didn't include her.

My mother was a fair skinned woman, with a warm smile and a nice sense of humor long jet black hair petite frame. She loved to dance, could cook, and clean a house immaculately. She also enjoyed electronics everything she did had that woman's touch, the way she dressed us, our home, even if she wrapped a gift it looked professional.

Yup he lost out, for women who wanted his money, and sex, they weren't half the woman my mother is, yes she's still alive and sober enjoying Florida, and we talk all of the time. My daddy's gone, but he did leave a trail of women and children lost and confused, but me, my sister, and mom are alright, even after the stone stopped rolling.

Chapter
Three

She was only sixteen
(Sam Cooke)

Sweet sixteen, bring in the balloons, the flowers, rent the hall, and let's show off daddy's little girl in her new dress.

For some there was no daddy, no party ECT...

I remember the day I felt the whole impact of ghetto life weighing on my shoulders like a ton of bricks. It was as if my soul, my restless soul realized that mama was gone, runned off with her ghetto lover one day after school. I still loved her and needed her more than I had ever needed her in my entire life.

Your see I had a baby boy Lamont who I loved and adored, but I hadn't been taught the ways of a mother yet. I didn't know how to cook, shop, clean, budget my meager income, but she just left. Probably, like most women in the ghetto losing their man was just as strong as watching your young man or husband be sold off.

But by the grace of God I learned. This was coupled together with the decision never to leave my child for no reason. Their were the years before that, dealing with all forms of physical, mental, and emotional abuse as well.

The most painful thing during this dark time was looking at my ghetto lover and not feeling any connection to anyone after being rejected by my mom, dad and sister my immediate family.

So I tried to take my life. I remember as I started to pass out or go toward the light, I prayed to live, and God heard me, and when I awoke in the hospital all alone, I felt connected. God had heard my prayers to live and serve him if he revealed himself to me.

You see by the time I was fourteen and a half years old I had a son, by my first young ghetto lover. We had met at a party one night, till this day I don't quite remember how I found out about this particular house party in the projects I grew up in, probably a friend or something, but I remember that it was kind of dark, you know how they use to turn off the lights at those back in day house parties. Their were some chips and soda, maybe some alcohol, I'm not sure, you see I didn't need a drink to enjoy music, because I love to dance.

In my humble opinion alcohol didn't make people have more fun, my experience with alcoholics was first they'd laugh a lot, make jokes then if someone said something they didn't like or look at them in an uncomfortable way, immediately they'd turn flustered and sweaty, start swearing and throwing blows or getting thrown out of somewhere, so I decided that drinking wasn't for me.

I met by baby's daddy at this darkly lit party he was encircled by some girls cheering him on while he danced. It was like art watching him paint the floor with his smooth glides and his alluring gaze. I stood near the door as though I was waiting for some kind of trouble to break out. I mean they always did at home once everyone was feeling nice, I watched from a distance wishing inside myself that he would ask me to dance, I could never bring myself to boldly speak to guys for I was too shy, and well the other girls were as I thought prettier and more outgoing than I was. So I just stayed put until he finally had and opening and he glided pass me a couple of times then he stopped in front of me and held his hands out for me to join him. Oh now I felt so honored, and so self confident, because he chose me above all of the other girls.

The reason it is so important to ghet-to love yourself is, one shouldn't need someone else to validate you. I should have been feeling that he should be honored to dance with me, and that I'm just as good as he is or anyone else for that matter.

But, I was on cloud nine, and he knew it, forget that fact that we weren't properly introduced, we danced for about an hour, and we left to go to my house where mother was not home and wasn't on her way home until the next day or so. We kissed till sun up imagine that we kissed until the sun came up, "ghetto love".

He made me feel loved and adored just by his touch his eye contact and smile of approval. I hadn't realized then how hungry I was for love or the human touch, and even though we didn't make love for a month or two I finally felt something from another human being, besides being beaten or yelled at or just plain ignored.

I didn't know then why I didn't love myself, but, looking, back I realize that, the only looks I got from my parents was either non- expressive, hard stares, or bitter angriness. Our parents then were starving for love from each other, or their parents. I see now though, they gave me what they could, but they had an empty account of love, and I had gotten use to this neglect to the point that I was only attracted to the kind of guys that expressed outward shows of adoration towards me, and the guys that didn't show this flare or have the time to spend emotionally cheering me up or catering to my low self esteem I had no need for them.

   My upbringing in the ghetto made me so self centered you see I had to get mine. I didn't care about money or material things, because this took to much time away from nursing my emotional wounds. I wanted my lovers attention twenty four hours a day. So they ran to the streets, to other women that were more stable and less controlling.

   I couldn't for the life of me figure out why they always ran from me, and yet they'd stay with me in the relationship for years. I mean by my trying to cater to their needs by cooking, baking, ironing, being polite, I can see why they preferred to be with me, I mean who else would cater to their every whim, but I didn't allow my relationship to breathe if anything I sucked the life right out of them.

   I did this until we were exhausted, just depleted all

of the body and soul out of them and myself. They got tired of feeling that they owed me something, you see I wasn't going to cheat, yell, scream, or ask or demand anything from them and they didn't give me anything.

After the first few months into the relationship they were already tired of me and my demands for this pure, perfect, and most sanctified of all life, our relationship.

When I didn't receive what I expected in return then, I would resort to yelling, swearing, and fighting, um sound familiar?, yeah, my childhood repeating itself. They all screamed for space, I think they wanted to be outer space. I just wanted to be loved and they did love me but, I didn't love myself so, exhausted and confused, and feeling let down by parents, siblings, and friends I decided that I didn't want to live, but like I've learned most feeling aren't positive, but negative and therefore probably not true.

I truly had a block, a wall inside of me that I couldn't knock down with one blow. But it had to come down brick by brick, sometimes I'd take down a brick, then put two more up, this would go on for *years until I could ghet-to love myself.*

Chapter
Four

Starting all over again is Gonna be Rough
(The Manhattans)

Ghetto Love is a peculiar thing, no one really knows how to express themselves positively, you have the quiet syndrome, where we simply say nothing or it's just the opposite just yelling and screaming, swearing, and fighting, yeah, imagine that.

I guess I've experienced a little too much of both, my mom and dad could never talk to each other, neither one of them really listened to each other. Looking back I know my dad was dead wrong, come on after he worked all week, he'd come home ready to go partying without mom, whom I guess he thought didn't deserve a break.

I mean she only cooked, cleaned, waxed floors, wash, dried, and folded the clothes, doctors appointments, the normal run of the millwork. You know what they say woman's work is never done.

Well getting back to the subject of rebuilding, considering no one came to see me in the hospital at least no one in my family. there was one person who I'll never forget, they know who they were. That was the one time I felt connected to someone. I guess it was the words of that caring person along with the way they looked at me, as if my dying would have affected them severely.

It would have been nice if my ghetto lover would have showed up, but I didn't see him until I came back to that depressing project apartment and all of my childhood pains and my present relationship , was a bit to much to handle.

After seeing the non-reaction from my family, it was time to make a change, a couple of months maybe four, but it was a nice change, somewhat of a spiritual change. Remember I made a promise to God, if he would let me live I would serve him, and although I've stumbled a few times, but he's the one I think of morning, noon, and night....

And I know He thinks of me.

After getting my GED and clerical training, I landed a job in the multiservice office in my neighborhood, even though my separation anxiety made me stay with my ghetto lover.

My whole life I sort of felt I was similar to a trapeze artist, jumping from one relationship to another. Just before letting go of one man I immediately swung to another man. I now realize this was as dangerous as swinging from one swing to another swing in mid air.

There was a youthful fight and optimism of fantasy inside my mind, that one day I'd find or build the perfect family, you know a family where the dad worked a 9 to 5, came home to a loving wife, who'd prepared dinner, washed clothes, cared for the children, and we'd all be so, so happy.....yeah right.

My optimisms though did help me see the sun each day, also feeling the warmth of my children's smiles and enjoy their laughter, they don't know till this day how they saved my life. They were my reasons for living, Eisha, George, Beverly, Benjamin, Phyllis, Andreisha, Stephanie, and my firstborn Lamont. Leprayer, Jeremiah, and Emmanuel my children from my second husband. My faith was also the foundation on which I built my new start.

I guess that's the reason I love music, it always seems to express those thoughts and feelings I wished my ghetto lovers would have said to me. So here's the reason for naming each chapter after a particular song. Each night I listen to slow jams from back in the day. I want to attribute this book to all of the artist, lyricist, and the performers who brought these melodious rhythms together to give me hope. I felt as if someone, somewhere was romantic, gentle, and

in tuned to my feelings. The words of a love song rather it's sung by Joe, one of my favorite artist or Carl Thomas, Charlie Wilson, Earth Wind and Fire's "Reasons" or the high tenor of Blood Stone, Stylistics or Barry Manilow's wholesome, breezy songs filling me with joy. It all made me feel that there is a world where love exist and is strongly expressed through musical lyrics.

The arts are and always will be a source of strength, because it's a positive form of expression, and communication, I find myself drawn to beautiful vases and glass design, animal, plant, sky, flowers, ect... to draw, carve or photograph it as we see them.

We live in a world filled with poets and writers who express themselves as life inspires them from within. What if for example my mother had taken the time to sing for she had a beautiful voice, or if she had pursued her dancing at the well known Elma Louis School in Massachusetts. Maybe she would have found her self-confidence, her dignity, or her inner beauty.

I heard it said "We are who we were" that means to

me that before this world bombarded us with it's cruelty, and it's desire to browbeat people to be what it wants us to be for profit or selfish gain, maybe we ,

all would have originally been strong cultured artist of various forms.

Some would have been carpenters with the ability to cut, smooth, design from wood everything from spoons to houses with great architectural beauty. Some would have weaved baskets for every sort of job or pleasurable decor. Then their are the potters who would have molded from their hearts pieces of crafted design. We would have the kind of validation we need to feel self love and a certain type of pride not the type of pride that is jealous, envious, and built on greed, or to be seen while shadowing someone else's accomplishments. In other words in a relationship their are two people that are equally created by a loving heavenly being, who through his creation has proved himself to be the master artist, the one whom we so earnestly try to immolate.

If two people love and respect that each one has and needs to be creative in one form of art or another they will give each other the time and space needed to fulfill that natural urge to create. The inner being the brain, heart, kidneys, all of these organs pump at a faster healthier rate when the desire inside us moves us to express our creativity, which is our true selves.

   Couples may have a common art, or they each may process an individual form of art but, if they don't respect and appreciate the others desire and need to follow their desire in peace it will create tension, pain, and inner torment.

   After all of the years of hurting and crying for love I've come to realize that this is the God given love inside each one of us, and we know we find we're drawn like bees to honey to certain forms of art, and it's up to us to give in and explore these natural yearnings, and express our selves to each other and then to the world.

               That's when we each will,
                  "Ghet-to Love"
                  Ourselves

Chapter
Five
If Loving you is Wrong I Don't Wanna be Right
(Gladys Night)

We can all look back on our past as children or young adults and recall the relationships of our moms, aunts, and grand mothers. it's not hard to remember the labor of these women. I recall an aunt whom I adored, how she laughed and loved music after a hard days work. I guess I'd always wondered how she came to be with my uncle, you see he stayed home all day drinking and try to get with all the women in the family young and old, and yet she stayed with him. This man was belligerent towards my aunt, I mean just rude.

Then their was my grandmother worked five days a week cleaning houses in the suburbs and caring for their children, and a wonderful southern cook, yet she had to endure the cheating flirting, and vain ways of my grandfather. He was a huge guy with a loud voice I mean the man just had a huge personality, not to mention the fact that he was a sharp dresser just beyond the normal alligator shoes and coats, snake shoes, snake coats, Bonneville's each year brand new, what's right, what's wrong, when you see two people work hard, has plenty of friends, yet ...I saw them alone when the other was not in view cheat on one another yet they stayed together till he died. My grandmother went through something I never seen

before or think I will ever see again you see she mourned like I never witnessed anyone before, she wouldn't throw away any of his clothes or move his room from they day he died she didn't really clean the house it's like time stopped for her, everything but the drinking.

Who really knows the relationship between two people except them. I have to come to this conclusion that it's only wrong when the pain in a relationship is something that (you) can't bare, you can't sleep for long periods of time, nightmares not able to focus on your children, then you must reconsider what is your priority in this life.

Like in my dedication to pain in the beginning of this book, had it not been for the pain in my life I wouldn't be the woman I am now.

My pain changed me, taught me things about myself my weaknesses my strengths, my creativity and how I thrive from pain. Pain isn't something to run from but pain is a teacher, I was so angry at sixteen, I wanted to dye. Angry about my upbringing, ghetto lovers, both mine and others, my financial situation, which hasn't changed much, still to a degree even my money problems brought out the beast in me the natural gift of being an entrepreneur. When you're born to a depressed mom, and a wandering father,

you take that pain and turn your lemons into lemonade, or in my case after my ghetto lover spent his earning on using. I looked into my refrigerator and turned twenty plums into a small fruit stand, this started me on my road to being an entrepreneur and owning my own businesses. So this took away the fear of new ventures in businesses self owned.

Pain made me work and do what I had to so my child and myself could survive. Washed clothes in the suburbs, iron clothes, cashier, flip burgers, till I decided I didn't want the pain of my past, present or future to make me endure the pain of working for someone else. Maybe I thought they could tell I was depressed, I could always feel what people felt about me I thought at first it was my imagination, but they could tell I never ever felt equal or as good as anyone else. This isn't hard to believe because I had no foundation in my family, financially or spiritually.

When you don't receive love it's damn hard to show it ... but, I seen too many women fall into a real bitter person. Why did I vow not to be bitter? I don't know why but, I do know I didn't like these women all. I've always have strived to never let anyone person determine who I was to become as a whole person. I'm not saying that they didn't affect me, but I wasn't going to let them make me evolve into a say what's on my mind no matter who it hurt, waiting to exhale,

burn the clothes type of a female. I wanted to focus on my schooling, my children, my creativity, and my creator.

"If loving you is wrong, I don't Wanna be right"

My mistake was staying in relationships that caused me so much pain I found myself repeating generations of hanging in there when I know I wasted so much time, decades hoping, dreaming, that I would be loved by my ghetto lover.

These ghetto lovers are blinded to the realities of working, sharing, commitment, self sacrifice, a spirit of husband and fatherhood, for they to can't produce something they've never experienced growing up.

but....

When they smile or dance you across the floor of sing you a song, write you a poem, you begin to see a godly side of them that attracts you and the world to them. it's a genetic gift of descents of kings without their thrown or tribe, and when we made love it's like nothing you've experienced, yes I've been made love to by the descendants of kings that's why so many women

sing,
            "If loving you is wrong I don't
                Wanna be right"

I've been made love to by descendants of kings
True warriors of life enduring years of pain

Pure is their spirit when they're in love with you
They can lift your soul whenever your feeling blue

Rich in color, movement and plenty of style
A touch or a smile can make your heart burn with fire

A physique so entwined with muscle and royal blood
Words so eloquent, smooth and endearing these all
put together moves you to rub

I've been made love to by descendants of kings
Richly rewarded by their royal offspring

They don't need money, riches, or fame
For they set the standards for the copiers to maintain

Theirs is the lightening you hear before thunder
Their voice is filled with wisdom, and truth of the
creator

From their head to their toes you make me a better to
be, because

"I've been made love to by the descendants of kings"
                By Phyllis Washington

Chapter
six

Diamond in the Back
Diggin the scene with a Gangster Lean

As a people we never had very much in the ghetto, thing hard to obtain, a good pair of converses, a good meal, a descent apartment, or a house whoa, that's going to far.

We weren't given good jobs, and if we got good jobs it was hard living in a structured environment, especially if you had a family similar to mine. A lot of cheating, drinking moms, fighting, yelling, swearing, or abuse which was mistaken for discipline, I'm not saying that we don't need a little discipline for these youth today, but maybe with a little balance, after all wasn't beating instituted during slavery? You know a good whipping and a lot of fear and you could get most slaves to grant your every wish.

Now it's time to get a job, oh yeah that seems a bit

far fetched considering out side of the ghetto their was a whole other world, you know similar to the welfare or state offices places that you experienced severe discrimination, well that's similar to what you feel on a job interview back in the day.

What's a "Diamond in the Back"?, This is a diamond shaped window in the back of old caddy's, or other luxury cars.

This began a whole era for our people in the ghetto. You might ask yourselves or at least I did when I saw these in my neighborhood. I mean if you one of these cars add some whitewall tires you could go and dig the scene and be dug. I wondered where did these ghetto superstars find the money to afford these luxuries?

None of the sistas had these luxuries but, they could afford a small ride around the block for a few small favors. Well when the brothas realized that they could get these cars and win the affections of the young sistas who also never experienced these personal attentions it was on and poppin.

"digging the scene with a gangster lean"

See you could sit in straight in these cars you had

to dig the scene.

   And oh what a scene it was to see. It looked like a circus to me but, others were totally fascinated with whole scene. Personally I was more intrigued with the person who could master the horn, or some other form of creativity, maybe riding his bike to class, you know taking knowledge of his culture. Even poetry, I've fell in love with poets here and there. It's not very often you'll see a brotha express what's inside of him, I guess only he knows how he feels in this land of the free, uh, free to be locked up, searched, or beaten.

   This was definitely a nee era for the ghetto, it's funny how human beings are I mean how one race seems to imitate another so often we immolate the very one we claim to loathe or even hate.

   In the ghetto so many brothas and sistas wanted to act or be like the white race, I remember watching the Brady Bunch seeing the house, the car the furniture the maid and some how admiring Carol Brady, the way she was always calm, happy secure, or seeing other white women with their long golden hair and their perky breast where as mine seemed to just drop. I mean I was a small framed full sized sista who got plenty of looks, and my share of honking cars, but it wasn't enough to take me out of the ghetto. I had to go to school and get pretty fed up with the whole idea of entering my project hallway, and seeing someone using it for a hang out or a bathroom. Yeah number one and two. I mean seeing my neighborhood about how you didn't need television just look out of the window, and you had all of the entertainment you needed.

and yet...

I knew white women who immolated us sistas, the way we talked, the way we dressed, then came after our fine African kings.

On the flip side the brothas were very envious of the white men, well they never wanted to dress like them or act like them, but envy came of what these white men had, money, houses, jewels, jobs, and cars.

I stressed the cars because getting a house was almost impossible because he would need a job, and that was out of the question because he needed and education and due to living situation and no money the brothas didn't want school. Some did that were in the ghetto, but the majority wanted some comfort first and once they found some comfort through their hustle, well you know their was no need for edumacation.

their was one thing they could get hands on and that was a car. Ask Fifty Cents, in his movie "Get Rich or Dye Trying", he got his hustle on and got him some wheels, then it seemed as though he got some dignity, some recognition. Even the women were ready to give up some play. Not that the brothas ever had a problem with that but, it was now easier to catch up with two or three at the same time. Yes even the game changed he could get his hustle on, you know keep up with his girls on the street skip out on his wife. I mean going to the store would take an half hour, now he could go to the store and check out his girl on the side in the same amount of time.

Cars a wives nightmare, you won't find the brothas driving no station wagon, I know my dad wouldn't be caught dead in one of those boats as we use to call them. See these weren't for " the wife", you see she couldn't be in no red convertible or a Benz, or a Cadillac with " Diamond in the Back".

Chapter Seven

A Change is Gonna Come
(Sam Cooke)

Million man walk or march I should call it. Hundreds of thousands of brothas marched to the capitol, Washington D.C., our people have marched for equal rights, to end segregation, to be taught in the schools and colleges to sit in the front of the bus and so on,

but...

Why did the brothas feel the need for million man march? We sistas didn't tell them to go, but, they went. Maybe too many fathers, sons, and grandfathers, have been on lock down and on drugs, or lacking the desire to be educated in the learning facilities. It maybe the jobs that weren't available for them...

Everybody wanted a change, mothers, daughters, wives, and sons. As adults we set the standards for the youth to follow how can I put it so you'll feel me? by the time I was thirteen years of age I had a baby son a year later his dad was incarcerated in an adult prison for four to eight years, mom was gone with her ghetto lover. I'd been molested, beaten, with shoes, extension cords, seen way too many knife fights at home between my parents, seen racial discrimination, been teased, ridiculed, and suffered ghetto itis. My dad was living the good life his money was for him, his personal pleasures cars, women gambling, and other vices, which meant their wasn't enough money for " the wife' and the kids,

Later I realized that I wasn't the only one experienced these pains but, some had it a lot worst, imagine that. Yes their was a whole race, generation just lost ,but , now they were our parents.

Values needed to change
loyalty to marriage, to jobs, to children, to self.

I have come to see that theirs a serious sickness amongst our people. I call it "looking out for number one", "numero uno", " the head hauncho".Why do I call that a sickness? Well,I found that when you say what's up to a brotha or a sista it can mean how you doing or can I borrow a few dollars. I guess the point I'm getting at is we as a people never connect with one another unless we want something from each other. "It's a shame the way you mess around with your mess". I have a lot of whys in this chapter, here's another one, why can't we be free to love, free to give, free to care about one another, without looking for a hook up or something?

Why?....

I don't have the answers to these questions but, I do realize that if we don't ask why were in serious denial. You must ask this of yourself and sometimes of others who can handle even hearing the questions. I'm no authority on these matters but, I do ask because, I don't want to stop living, caring, or loving, because you can't.

I want to be free to do these things completely, without fear that you might hurt me or take advantage of my kindness. When we're able to love, live, and care freely without wanting something in return I feel

that......

"A Change is gonna come"
not from the MAN but, from
US.

Weeze Free

Free to do what...
Slavery ended, we were free
To do what ever we wanted
Free to;
sleep
Wake-up
Marry
Work Learn ect...
I'm relatively young never been a slave or have I,
Slave to welfare, to wrong decision
Choices
 Never being free from birth then,
One day it was over
 What would we do now
 Having no money. ,

          Home
            Education
              Nameless
                Culture stripped

Did being free enslave us more
Enslaved to have to
Make money by whatever means necessary,
Washing clothes   For the whites
Cleaning house   For the whites
Babysitting   For the whites
Cooking   For the whites

For little or no money

For little or no food

Called girl even though
I was the legal age of a woman
Called boy even though
I was at the legal age of a man

Weeze Free

Where's my heritage
                    My dad
                     My mother
                    My grandmother
                    My grandfather
                    My family
You sold me
everything I knew you told me
You were very bold to me
 You did everything, but hold me

Weeze Free

Now you give me projects decorated
with trees
Welfare, food stamps, and you call me lazy

Weeze Free

My grandfather had no chance to
Have the things yours did
 He had no schooling and some did
Have the chance to educate themselves
And attend school at a very high price
Maybe he was the only one of his
Kind in the school
Maybe he had to work extra hard
To get where he got but it was
Worth it to him to give back something

To his family what was taken,
COULDN'T READ, COULDN'T WRITE
COULDN'T TALK, COULDN'T FIGHT
We could pray and God sent us
Some light
Harriet
Martin
Douglass to name a few
These understood what
being free meant
To have ones name stand for
Something
It didn't matter what they called us
Kunta-Toby
Kizzy
Fredrick, Daniel or George or Rosa
It was what that person stood for
Equal rights, Family value

Weeze Free

Some led us to freedom
Some invented things from peanuts
Some wrote about change of the treatment
of one another
Some were hanged lynched, or sold
To keep us together
To help us read
To teach us our rights

Weeze Free

Segregation
Yours, mines
Your entrance, My entrance
Your fountain, My fountain
Front of the bus, back of the bus
Your side of town

My side of town
Your school, my school, north, south
Weeze Free

How do you get away from the pain and hurt
Crushed spirit, from being treated like dirt
Can't give you what others had
To may wife, my children your making me mad
Free to me is just a word
You five, you take your making life so hard
Desegregation
Thrust together like oil and water
It only makes gray
The color of the sky before a storm
and the storm did come
Riots, dogs and water hoses
They said we wanted to much
To read
To write
To learn
To earn
To live

Weeze Free

Some took time to read and write
Some took time to stand strong and fight
Some took time to stand strong and fight
Some ran from this slavery into the night
Guided by God, guided by moonlight

But what about the ones who were
Crushed in spirit from beatings
                              From rape
                              From imprisonment
                              From isolation
What did freedom mean for his son
The second, third and forth generation

he took time to sleep
          Time to linger
          Time to play
Time to drink
Dinking, drugs, whores and thugs
Gold, silver, chains, and lugz
Free to sit and stare
Claiming life's to hard and it isn't fair

Weeze Free

Is freedom taken for granted today
O I must ask myself
So many died so I could read so I could write
Freedoms not young it's not old
Freedom's a frame of mind a matter
of ones free will to chose his or her
coarse in life whether it be good or bad

Weeze Free

Free man
Free woman , wife
Free husband
Free child, or free teen
Free mother, free dad
Boss, employer, employee, ect...
You get my drift

Weeze Free

Free to treat each other in the way the golden rule
states in the bible, do unto others as you would have them do
unto you.
It's very simple to apply, we all want love, respect, honor equal
rights for ourselves, and our families.
Being free means that it's up to us individually to decide how
we're going to behave on a daily basis to our neighbors.

Those who have more of anything than their neighbor should give of themselves in whatever gift go has endowed to them.
Then we'll learn the true meaning of being free.
It's up to you to decide what that is and how you can express your freedom

Weeze Free
Written By
Phyllis Washington

Chapter
Eight

Slow Jams
All old School
(Baby Face)

Barry White, Delphonics, Spinners, Harold Melvin and the Blue Notes, Blue Magic, Temprees, just to mention a few.

" Walking in the Rain with the One I Love" "I love You, You Love me", "I Love Music" , (Yes but, I do love music).

Music can make you cry, it can make you happy, or cal, you down. This has been a source of comfort for me the last decade of my life. Not that I don't like the new school music I've heard a few great inspirational pieces such as Tupac's "Dear Mama", and, " Keep your Head Up". Yeah it just gives me strength to go on, just knowing that something else can relate and a man, but, maybe I should say a son, but that's another book.

Getting back to sloooow Jammms, what can I say the lyrics to these melodies were able to let you and you and your ghetto lover "Just get it On". It was a form of escape, fantasy world where everything on the outside world just didn't matter for an hour or two.

Musical lyrics echoed life in the ghetto, but slow jams brought everything to a halt, boy. I'm gonna miss Barry Whites " I'm gonna love you, love you, love you just a little bit more". It was that coupled together with his Love Unlimited Orchestra. Just to see a black man from the ghetto have an orchestra that size just blew me away. We all loved his deep baritone voice. It made it seem as though he was right in the room with you.

What about Blood Stone with " Natural High " or Earth Wind and Fire's " Reasons" so moving. Let's face it these songs even today are a breathe of fresh air, especially when we hear so much thug loving songs. I only with that the brothas today will continue to use part of these songs or melodies to inspire then to write songs and music so inspirational of life and their by preserve what love is.

Slow jams speak about the hurt of a break up. Chi-lites put it well with "Have you Seen Her" remember Blue Magic's " Spell", or Black Ivory's " Just because of

You"? Um Um.

" Stop Look Listen" by the Stylistics. The writer's telling you to " Listen to your heart hear what it's saying Love", a master piece. I could go on and on, I think I've made my point.

Their are only a " One in a Million" chance that you'll find true love in which you will " Stay" together and you'll look back and " Remember the Time" when you fell in love and "Ooooh Ooooh Baby Baby" the passions of " Sweet Love".

So I encourage you to play slow jams everyday whether your with someone or your enjoying yourself, you'll still feel the love and hopefully,

"Ghet- to Love Yourself"

Chapter
Nine

A Penny for Your Thoughts
(Tavares)

" you got me going in Circles" this ghetto life. Just try coping from day to day. Everyday something new. Some days their were enough police in the neighborhood to start a small war, then the addicts, prostitutes fights over men, and over woman.

As a child I watched this whole scene not just from the outside looking in but, right in my own home. Lots of drinking, swearing, and a lot of invidiousness. Envy wretched havoc on our neighborhoods. Why? I don't know, none of us had much of anything. I mean we lived in tiny cubicles called a-part-ments, yes it a part of a brick wall.

And don't even mention the roaches the warden I mean the housing manager had the place exterminated once a year, unless your apartment needed to be bombed. At that time you had to stay outside for at least six to eight hours, then come back and open all of the windows just to breathe. Neither way worked the roaches came right back.

My thoughts were just mingled with fear, jealousy, low self esteem. When your not validated as a youth by your parents nothing no one says can lift you out of this for a long time. I mean it took years before I felt special. What changed my thinking was when I took the focus off myself and put it on helping and assisting others.

Ironic the lessons life teaches you over time. Yeah all those sayings come to mind, live and learn. Which is one of the hardest ways to learn, because it means that you'll receive a lot of pain this then you learn from the mistake usually because it hurts so much. Kind of like being burned it doesn't take long before one realizes that you don't want to feel that heat again.

Some through prison, learn that crime doesn't pay. Yeah some go again and again like ghetto love you stay when we probably should have gone a long time ago. You've been lied to, cheated on, abused verbally the list goes on and on, but we can't seem to walk away. I know I've been there, " Parents Love Your Children"!!!!

As I think back, since now I have some sense I never took the time to meditate, really analyze my relationships before, I got deeply involved with someone. It's really sad, that my childhood was so filled with violence and fighting, along with feeling unconnected to anyone that the first man or boy that seemed just a flicker of happy or confident had my attention.

I thought oh he must be strong, secure, and a good person, not even knowing that the brothas were more afraid, and self conscious than us sistas were. For good reason they had no doe, been looking their fathers and if they knew where they was, it was jail or at another woman's house.

sad, huh?

I have an uncle who doesn't till this day know his father is, yeah never met him. How or what that does to a brotha I don't know, then theirs the step dad who've stepped to the plates, like walking into an oncoming bullet not being accepted, or something like some step mothers full of jealousy and hate because of the genetic bond and similarity of the ex-spouse. How can we ever win with these odds against us. Weary as a race trying to love, or be loved, or just running from love and commitment altogether. Feeling as hell what's the use in getting up, putting up another fight today?

No it ain't easy, yeah I said ain't because it ain't easy at all, but, it is worth it because like I said in the beginning of my book pain isn't the enemy it is our teacher and if we pay close attention we can learn from it. The way pain acts, the way pain is always unexpected, not really, pay close attention.

Pain can even make you think your crazy, loosing, it Yeah just insane, but that's ok if you step back and " Let go and Let God". I've been taught this through Alanon Anonymous. What does this mean to me? Well that you'll find that in life you don't have control over your children's life or behavior once they reach a certain age but, life goes on, you can't control your parents, their treatment of you or of themselves, but life does and will ever unfoldingly go on.....

Let God....

Yes let God deal with your problems, your parents, your ghetto lover, your children, when we practice this and or concepts like it we free ourselves from doing God's job.

So, at one time my life was a blur, or a dream like state but, now maybe you'll pay a penny for my thoughts and I'll "Pay a Penny for your Thoughts".

Chapter Ten

We've Weathered the Storm
(Phyllis Washington)

"Can you stand the rain" by New Edition, " I Wanna go outside in the Rain" by the Delphonics, and more "Under my Umbrella" by Rhianna. Many have song these lyrics to express themselves while in relationships. To reveal the pain in their hearts to their lovers, wives, and husbands.

I wrote this particular song during a trying period in my marriage and it has been a source of inspiration to me and my husband ever since. Sometimes in a relationship we experience stormy weather. It could be financial, in the ghetto this is a major problem for many. We have seen our ghetto lovers struggle with this aspect of life. Going for job interviews at the local gas stations, burger joints, or a nearby supermarket. I know this was hard for the brothas, due to the fact that the local drug dealer was pulling in more money an hour than this brotha might make in a week. This had to be hard to endure for a couple trying to make it with a child or two.

I've seen my ghetto lover try to do whatever they could do to provide food, pampers, and rent. This definitely brought about stormy tides in our relationship. Some of them felt they had to sell drugs, commit acts of crime in order for us to survive. Most of their fathers weren't in their lives to guides them through the stormy times. Just losing my mother at an early age was devastating. I can't imagine the hurt and pain these young brothas felt not knowing their biological fathers. Talk about having the world on your shoulders. Compassion comes into play for all to share not only for these brothas but, also for their women and children.

Many feel well why didn't they plan their families, or think these things through before they went and got some woman or girl pregnant? This book is to help give you some understanding about the ghetto and the mind set of the people in the hood. So don't sit their judging, or feeling as though if it were you it would have been different. Maybe, but youth like myself had experienced nothing but abuse since birth. Have witnessed fighting in and out of the house, cheating, poverty, molestations, never talked calmly to, just yelling and screaming.

I remember running out of the house scared for my life, from my mother in a drunken rage. I know now that she had a dis-ease that occurred after her mom died. When my mother was only seven years old. She was passed on to family members who also drank and she also blamed herself for her mothers death. See she was always told that she was a bad little girl and so when her mom died she thought it was her fault. A vicious cycle in my family. It was one I was determined to STOP!

Yes, life in the ghetto was often like a cyclone, tornado, or a Tsunami. My head like others was in a whirlwind half of the time. So the need for affection was like a dessert land without water. An oasis was our love for our ghetto lovers, at least that's how it was for me. Yeah, some may say I should have waited for love till I was older but, those times with my ghetto lover was a life line in stormy times.

Just to have some one to hold me and caress me was well over due even as a child I imagined strongly about what making love like. Why, I only can say that my parents were their for me, even a little more than they were maybe I would have had a different destiny. Many of us children from the ghetto didn't have anyone to acknowledge our strengths. For instance now that I have a little more control over my choices in life and some peace I'm realizing as time goes by. And even though I must share my time with my children and husband I still motivate myself to explore these strengths and creativities in myself and others.   And I'm enjoying it......

We in the ghetto had a community though that had mothers, grandparents, cousins, and schools. We all knew each others families, and we even called each other aunty, uncle, mom, even if this was just a neighbor. Maybe they all drank together, and fought together we all got up the next day family. We knew it was the poverty we all shared in this ghetto life.

So we didn't plan our families, but once we had these children it sort of made some of us wake up seeing and feeling we sure didn't want our children to experience this kind of upbringing. Many went to school, college, and like myself got good jobs. I truly miss this part of my life and the times when things started to change. I miss the outreach programs that were available to us youth. There were GED programs, job training, and this was free to any who tool advantage of them.

Now looking back, no one was at fault not my mother, father, or my ghetto lover. I see clearly that we were all victims of a system that meant us to hate, and envy one another. By keeping us broke, hungry, and uneducated, their was only one coarse we all could take and that was to attack one and love whomever we could.

I heard it said by many who have over came this ghetto- itis to stop hating one another, STOP blaming one another, and STOP looking for someone else to take responsibility for your confusion. I won't say your mistakes but, your confusion.

JUST STOP!!!!

It's time to LOVE one another, LOVE our brothas, LOVE our sistas, LOVE our mothers, LOVE our fathers, and Pleasssssssssssse

"Weather the Storm"
with one another

WE'VE WEATHERED THE STORM

Dedicated to my loving husband
Daniel Washington

The sky was dark gray and ominous
Their were so many dark clouds were the formed just for us

It rained it pored so hard on our faces
We held each other so tight so life wouldn't erase us

You slipped into a puddle and I pulled you up
I prayed so hard I couldn't stop crying I was fed up

I saw you try to dry off from all the rain
I got wet to from the great pain

The clouds are clearing for you and me
I saw the sun on your face you had grown like a tree
Your arms are branches so long and so lean

Giving me shade when life did me so wrong
Now we're a garden from which to eat
Our children our friends fid our love so sweet

One with the universe the sun, moon, the stars
So now where ever we are the sun shines

By,
Phyllis Washington

Chapter
Eleven

Hero
(Mariah Carey)

" Theirs a hero if you look inside your soul", some of us had to find this out the hard way. I know that's how it was for me. Most of my greatest achievements in life were found by trial and errors. I remember the first time I tried to learn African braiding, by a lovely African woman who lived in Boston, Massachusetts. She allowed me to come to where she was working and sit with her and the other talented stylist from Africa, and I was amazed not only with the speed of their braiding but, the perfection with which they braided. So I went home to practice this craft and realize I did something very different and I don't think I've ever seen anyone do this since. You see my braids all spiraled. This was good because, to spiral braids you had to take a client and drape them with numerous towels then take rollers and curl the braids, and then lean them back over a bowl of very hot water and then pour spoons of this hot water on each braid.

Well this chapter isn't about braiding but, it is how theirs a hero inside of each of us. I attended cosmetology school in the early 90's. I had done some sales in cosmetics, I got into this for the money and later found out that it made me feel good about myself. Imagine that, just sitting with others teaching them to look and feel good about themselves. Imagine that, just sitting at a kitchen table with a mother, left home with her children, a little bored or tired from washing, cooking, or other chores mothers do. She tries my products and sees a new person in the mirror, or maybe the person she was before marriage or parenthood.

The one thing I learned from selling cosmetics was I could make money on my own schedule, look good, and do the same for others.

My next purpose in this book is to help you to Ghetto Love yourself. I have had my days of low self esteem and feeling just like giving up. See God has another purpose for us and that's to be happy. It doesn't matter to God where you come from or what status in life your in right now, He's there and wants to help us.

I don't mean to seem preachy but, I've been watched over all of my life. I now realize this. Many of us that if it weren't for God we would be dead. If not from the streets, bad parents, or just cashing in our own chips. Just always remember as sung by

Nancy Wilson, "What a Difference a Day Makes", this is so true.

Each day is another opportunity to grow, change, and or teach. Some days I find that I do one of each or all three. One thing about life your going to grow. Whether you want to or not like a flower once the seed is planted the sun hits it and the rain comes it's gonna grow. Life is gonna teach you what ever your parents didn't. If you pay attention to the mistakes of others you'll learn, even if no one is their to teach you constructively.

Change is something that's gonna happen. You don't survive this kind of tough lesson without the grace of God, but as I think about it God knew what I what I needed to survive in this world. so he allowed me to experience these things to strengthen my weaknesses. I was always afraid especially at night, afraid of confrontation even if it meant standing up for myself. Never wanted any committed schedule, I was already stressed out way before I turned twenty - one years of age. This was suppose to be the age of adulthood when I was prepared for life. Nope not in the ghetto, by that age I felt like a forty year old woman, but when I looked into the eyes of my children I knew that whatever childhood I was suppose to have was gone. IT WAS THEIR TURN......

Teacher………

Teach and be taught in my case, remember in the last chapter when I spoke of family in the ghetto? Well their was a woman whom I'll never forget Ma Beatty they called her. This woman was vibrant in everyway, she cooked some of the best food in the projects. You could see her clothes hanging from the building to the nearest tree or pole, nice clean white sheets blowing in the sun from a pulley. If you were hungry or homeless you could go to Ma Beatty for a hot meal and some good gossip. She also came to my aid many times, when my ghetto lover got locked up, and when my distressed mother left me with a baby boy. I must take this time again to thank her she was a mother to me then, teaching me to cook, clean and sterilize baby bottles for my little Lamont, my baby boy.

Their were others to that I thank who were in the projects that offered assistance for whom I am grateful. After going to school and obtaining a job things started to look up for me. I taught my children to do the same to get their education and work hard either for themselves or for a business. I didn't forget to instill the words of the bible in my children and to let them know the power of God in our lives and to give thanks for everything.

That was along time ago, but I don't regret anything in my life, because I know that everything I did was for my children and for that I'm grateful. Their were a lot of tears, due to the fact that I didn't know half of what I was doing, but everyday I got up with a prayer and renewed vision to "keep on keeping on".

Since that time I've learned to love myself and to instill this in my children. I've given plays with the youth in Massachusetts.

I sincerely want all everywhere to get to know that theirs a hero inside of themselves. Sometimes we have the needed support from parents or other loving guardians, but even if you don't always remember that it's right inside of you, just listen to your God given senses it will lead you in the right path, the path to.........

GHET-TO
YOURSELF

GHET-TO
LOVE
Yourself

Growing up in the ghetto, was quite an experience for a young girl of seven years old. The whole era during that time was one of trying to make ends meet each day.

It was also a time of enduring the pain of distressed parents, left deserted and abandoned by a husband or a wife. We children became the victims of the times in the ghetto.

This book is to give some insight into the ghetto life, that I was raised through. It also speaks of the pain I suffered, and yet how the pain became a teacher to me.

I hope you'll read this with an open mind, compassion, and be inspired to face the challenges you face at work, home, raising a family, in these especially hard times , and realize that you can ghet-to love yourself.

For information to purchase this book and hear of my other books coming soon E-mail me at becomewon@yahoo.com or call 774-219-3247

Printed in the United States
by Baker & Taylor Publisher Services